A WALLACE-HOMESTEAD PRICE GUIDE

American Country STORE

DON & CAROL RAYCRAFT

Wallace-Homestead Book Company
Radnor, Pennsylvania

Published in Radnor, Pennsylvania 19089, by Wallace-Homestead,
a division of Chilton Book Company

Designed by Anthony Jacobson
Manufactured in the United States of America
Cover photo by Carol Raycraft

Library of Congress Cataloging-in-Publication Data
Raycraft, Don.
    The American country store / Don and Carol Raycraft.
      p.   cm.
    "A Wallace-Homestead price guide."
    ISBN 0-87069-723-4
    1. General stores—Collectibles—United States—Catalogs.
2. Antiques—United States—Catalogs.   I. Raycraft, Carol.
II. Title.
NK805.R36   1994
745.1'0973'075—dc20   94-11628
                                    CIP

1 2 3 4 5 6 7 8 9   3 2 1 0 9 8 7 6 5 4

American Country STORE

Contents

Acknowledgments   vi

Part One *Introduction*   **1**

  A Brief History of the American Country Store   4
  Chronology of Packaging, 5
  Dating Country Store Antiques by Patent Number, 6

  Buying Country Store Antiques   7
  Shops, 9
  Auctions, 9
     Buying at Auction, 9
  Finds, 10
  Flea Markets, 10
  Antiques Markets, 11
  Specialty Shows, 11

  Price Trends   12

  Resources   13

  Interview with Chris Fricker   13

Part Two *Picture Price Guide*   **15**

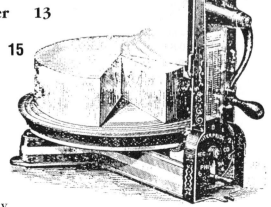

Acknowledgments

The authors appreciate the assistance of the individuals listed below in gathering material for this book. Without their invaluable help, this could not have been completed.

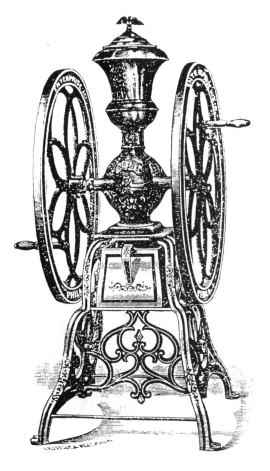

Opal Pickens

Dr. Alex Hood

Patricia McDaniel

Old Storefront Antiques

Darrell and Lana Potter

Ken and Carllene Elliott

Gary and Lorraine Boggio

Teri and Joe Dziadul

Chris Fricker

Ray and Nancy Gerdes

Kay and Dick Thompson

Bruce and Vicki Waasdorp

Jim White

PART ONE

Introduction

A major emphasis in the antiques books we have written over the years is to focus upon examples that collectors can still find. Some items will call for deep pockets and a lengthy hunt and others can be found tomorrow at the antiques mall on the corner.

In this book we have attempted to include a cross section of country store items from private collections and antiques shops that reflect a range of interests, specialities, and prices. Perhaps the items most desired by country store collectors today come from the 1880–1920 period. To concentrate on that time frame exclusively would have excluded some of the exceptional items from the 1930s through the 1950s found in this book.

We have collected country store antiques for almost twenty-five years. The problem has always been that we also collect decorated stoneware, textiles, painted furniture, Shaker, and folk art. If we had been intelligent enough early on to limit our horizons, our checking account balance would be imposing, our vehicles would still be under warranty, and our lives would be considerably less complicated.

In our travels across America we have encountered numerous country store collectors who are much more specialized than we have ever been. There are so many potential avenues to take for country store collectors that it is a full-time job just to keep semi-abreast of escalating prices in the myriad categories.

There are individuals who collect colorful tins that once held everything from soup to opium. Others have limited their pursuits to tobacco-related tins. Some seek only cylindrical tobacco tins manufactured by P. Lorillord and Co. of Jersey City, New Jersey, in the early 1900s. Many are content to add "pocket" tobacco tins to their collection and pay no attention to any other form.

We are convinced that almost everything ever commercially produced by a company or by someone in the United States is collected somewhere by somebody. These somebodies know the variations in packaging, dates of manufacture, and the relative value of whatever it is that they cannot live without. The search may be a lifelong pursuit or only a momentary hobby, but it usually becomes of paramount importance for the duration of the obsession.

It doesn't make any difference if the hunt is centered on "pocket" tobacco tins or early twentieth-century Pepsi-Cola bottles. For many of us the hunt itself is the primary joy of collecting, and the anticipation of finding the item is usually more satisfying than the actual discovery.

Recently we have been involved in two potentially significant "finds" that turned out to be dust rather than diamonds. Even though both misadventures were not rewarding experiences, they reconfirmed our belief that every lead should be vigorously pursued and great things can be found through serendipity.

Most of us have received telephone calls from someone's cousin's aunt's neighbor's best friend who heard at the beauty parlor that we collected "old tins" and had found one at a garage sale and "it might be for sale, but I have no idea what it is worth." Over the years we have periodically collected Shaker furniture and boxes. As Shaker prices have increased on the same growth curve as the national debt, our interest has waned to some extent. Recently, we received a letter from the friend of a man whose uncle had seen one of our Shaker books in a local library. The lady indicated in the note that her parents had been Shaker collectors since the 1930s and had a huge personal collection that they wanted to sell. She added that they had paid no attention to values over the years and would offer it to us "for whatever we thought was fair." The couple's daughter had graciously enclosed her home telephone number for our response.

For the next week we attempted in fifteen minute intervals to reach the daughter. With each failure to connect the anxiety level increased significantly. Finally on a Sunday evening at 11:00 p.m. the missing daughter answered her telephone. She had been out of town at a national rabbit breeders association meeting. She was pleased that we called because her parents were moving and wanted to dispose of the collection immediately. The remainder of the conversation went as follows:

Q. When can we see the collection?
A. Tomorrow or the next day would be convenient for us.

2

Q. How big is the collection?

A. They have about 3,000 pairs?

Q. Pairs? Pairs? Pairs of what?

A. Why, pairs of salt and pepper shakers.

If silence is golden, the pause that followed was worth more than all the gold in California.

Shortly after the salt shaker fiasco, we had a telephone call from a pharmacist who was retiring after working for more than forty years in a building that he owned. (The original drugstore had opened in 1923.) He wanted us to meet him at his business and go through the building to point out items that may have value to antiques collectors. The shelving and a variety of fixtures had been in place since the store had opened, almost seventy years previously.

If you are even a casual collector of store-related antiques or advertising, this type of invitation can inspire endless speculation about what might be in the attic or the basement. Was it possible that an unopened case of 1952 Topps baseball cards was stacked under the stairs by a careless stockboy while Harry Truman was president?

As it turned out, the tour of the facility and the basement resulted only in the purchase of an Ex-Lax thermometer that had been on the front of the building since Franklin Roosevelt was in the White House. The only other salvageable item of any appreciable age was a very collectible safe that was also incredibly heavy and almost impossible to separate from the store without removing the roof and importing a crane.

In the 1960s we lived in the rural central Illinois village of Hopedale. There was a surviving general store in the community called "Jingling's." Mr. Jingling, the founder of the business, was long deceased by this point but his two elderly daughters, neither of whom had ever married, managed the operation. As we look back on the situation, our naivete was overshadowed only by our ignorance of the opportunity that was presented to us. In every collecting career there will be a moment when you trip over an opportunity that may be outside your realm of experience. At that point sit back, do some research, or call in someone with more knowledge to assist you in the evaluation and decision-making process.

When Mr. Jingling died, his daughters continued to run the business and rarely, if ever, ordered new merchandise. (There was no reason to order new merchandise because the old merchandise seldom went out the door.) It was like a close out sale that lasted thirty years. The store was packed with clothing, hardware, gift items, canned goods, and a wide variety of other wares. Walnut spool cabinets, metal advertising signs, oak needle cases, seed boxes, a huge coffee grinder with a brass American eagle finial, and a host of other store fixtures from the 1920s through the 1940s were frozen in time. It appeared to us that the town and the Jinglings had a unique arrangement. The sisters came to work every morning, closed for an hour at noon, went home every evening at 5:05 p.m., and were seldom, if ever, bothered by customers.

As neophyte collectors we failed to grasp the potential of what had been placed before us. We attempted to purchase a spool cabinet, the coffee grinder, and some of the signs, but we were quickly informed that those items were part of the business and not for sale. We did not take the time to examine the merchandise that was available.

Christmas decorations, Halloween items, canned goods, tobacco-related collectibles, and sporting goods were passed over even though they maintained their original price tags from twenty to forty years before.

Several years after we moved from the community and the sisters had either died or entered a nursing home, an auction of the store's contents drew a large crowd of semi-serious collectors. Unfortunately, we found out about the auction three days after it was held.

A Brief History of the American Country Store

Anybody who grew up in America from the early 1900s through the 1950s had the opportunity to visit the corner "mom and pop" grocery store that sold soft drinks, penny candy, bread, lunch meat, and yesterday's newspaper. If you drank the bottle of Double Cola in the store, you didn't have to pay the 2¢ deposit. These stores offered credit, home delivery of groceries, and sometimes a part-time job after school that helped us pay off the tab we had accumulated when the new baseball cards came out each spring.

Most of these stores stayed in business because each one served a specific geographic section of town in established neighborhoods and there was not significant competition among other local grocery operations. Advertising expenses were almost nonexistent other than the sign hanging in front of the store.

The early country stores of the 1820–1865 period carried products that were either home grown or made within a few miles of the store. Barter was much more commonly used than cash in most transactions. There was not a wealth of manufactured products that were available to rural and small-town consumers. The local country store provided the primary opportunity for social interchange and sharing local gossip. Residents picked up their mail, sold their vegetables and honey, and ordered cloth for mourning clothes when a tragedy occurred.

Lifestyles began to change after the Civil War because the northern factories that had manufactured cannons and uniforms for a victorious army now turned to producing goods for a growing middle class with money to spend. The country store suddenly had competition from mail order catalogues that could offer goods to local consumers at competitive prices. It became very fashionable to decorate homes with furniture from Grand Rapids rather than locally crafted furnishings.

In 1916 Piggly Wiggly opened a self-service grocery store in Memphis that was the first of thousands to follow. In 1937 shopping carts were introduced to the grocery stores and hand-carried wire baskets were thrown away.

After World War II, improved "hard" roads and the increasing availability of automobiles continued to change America's buying habits. In 1950 if your mother sent you to the corner store for a jar of mustard, there were probably two varieties from which to make your selection. As the 1950s wore on, almost every community with a stoplight acquired a supermarket that stocked thousands of different products. The "mom and pop" stores could not possibly compete. Their product offerings were limited by a lack of shelf space and they bought in such small quantities that they could not survive in a marketplace now driven by price competition rather than service and customer loyalty.

As the owners of the corner groceries and general stores retired or died, their sons and daughters had no interest in attempting to sustain businesses that had no potential for growth or success.

Chronology of Packaging

1660s Paper packages were used to wrap medicines.

1680 An advertisement in a London newspaper suggested that customers bring a box if they want to purchase tea.

Late 1600s Wine bottles with specific tavern markings were in use in England and colonial America.

1750 Paper labels appeared on wine bottles.

1770s Pottery jars were used for hair dressings, mustard, and medicines.

1798 A papermaking machine was invented.

1800 Wooden boxes with paper labels were found in stores.

1809 A method of preserving food in glass bottles was introduced.

1820 New York City grocery stores offered oysters and salmon in glass bottles.

1840s Metal "tin" foil was used to wrap individual chocolates and packages of tea and coffee.

After 1850 Matches and match boxes were in daily use in most homes. Liquid ink in glass or stoneware bottles was available in stationery stores. Butter and cigarettes were wrapped in paper packages.

Early 1850s A patent was issued for a machine to make paper bags.

Late 1850s Cotton bags were used for packaging flour, but Civil War demands for cotton caused a shortage of cotton and merchandisers turned to heavy paper. By 1870, paper bags could easily hold 50–75 pounds of flour.

1856 Patents were issued to G. Borden for processing canned milk.

Early 1870s Paper bags were used by some stores for customers to carry home their purchases.

1970s "Flat" pocket tobacco tins were offered.

1873 Machines mass-produced paper bags; many more stores began to use paper bags.

1880 Packages of cigarettes had stiffeners added to keep the contents from being smashed. The stiffeners evolved shortly into the first baseball cards.

1896 A company in Evansville, Indiana, sold 500,000 bottle caps to Anheuser-Busch in St. Louis.

1898 The National Biscuit Company packaged its products in moisture-proof boxes for use at home. The country store cracker barrel was put in the attic. Kraft cheese was available in family-sized packages.

1899 Campbell Soup was offered in grocery stores across America for 10¢ a can.

1900 Paper, pottery, metal, foil, glass, and wood were commonly used by food manufacturers in packaging their products.

1910 Aluminum foil was available to consumers.

1912 Cellophane was initially utilized in packaging.

1935 Cone-top and flat-top beer cans were introduced.

1937 The shopping cart was found in grocery stores.

Late 1950s Large supermarkets replaced the neighborhood grocery store.

Dating Country Store Antiques by Patent Number

During the calendar year of 1859, the United States Patent Office issued patents numbered from 22,447 to 26,641 for product inventions or improvements. If an item has a patent number of 24,369, it dates from 1859. Keep in mind that a piece that carries the 1859 patent number could have continued to be made into the twentieth century with the same patent number if it was not redesigned or substantially altered. (Following information supplied by U.S. Patent Office.)

Year	Patent Number
1859	22,477
1860	**26,642**
1861	31,005
1862	34,045
1863	37,266
1864	41,047
1865	**45,685**
1866	54,784
1867	60,685
1868	72,959
1869	85,503
1870	**98,460**
1871	110,617
1872	122,304
1873	134,504
1874	146,120
1875	**158,350**
1876	171,641

Year	Patent Number
1877	185,813
1878	198,733
1879	211,078
1880	**223,210**
1881	240,373
1882	254,836
1883	269,820
1884	291,016
1885	**310,168**
1886	353,494
1887	355,291
1888	375,720
1889	395,305
1890	**418,665**
1891	443,987
1892	466,315
1893	488,976
1894	511,744
1895	**531,619**
1896	552,502
1897	574,369
1898	596,467
1899	616,871
1900	**640,167**
1901	664,827
1902	690,385
1903	717,521
1904	748,567
1905	**778,834**
1906	808,618
1907	839,799
1908	875,679
1909	908,436
1910	**945,010**
1911	980,178
1912	1,013,095
1913	1,049,326
1914	1,083,267
1915	**1,123,212**
1916	1,166,419
1917	1,210,389
1918	1,251,458
1919	1,290,027
1920	**1,329,352**
1921	1,364,063

1922	1,401,948
1923	1,440,362
1924	1,478,996
1925	**1,521,590**
1926	1,568,040
1927	1,612,790
1928	1,654,521
1929	1,696,897
1930	**1,742,181**
1931	1,787,424
1932	1,839,190
1933	1,892,663
1934	1,941,449
1935	**1,985,878**
1936	2,026,516
1937	2,066,309
1938	2,104,004
1939	2,142,080
1940	**2,185,170**
1941	2,227,418
1942	2,268,540
1943	2,307,007
1944	2,338,081
1945	**2,366,154**
1946	2,391,856
1947	2,413,675
1948	2,433,824
1949	2,457,797
1950	**2,492,944**
1951	2,536,016
1952	2,580,379
1953	2,624,046
1954	2,664,562
1955	**2,698,434**
1956	2,728,913
1957	2,775,762
1958	2,818,567
1959	2,866,973
1960	**2,919,443**

Buying Country Store Antiques

Country store-related antiques and collectibles can be found almost any-where, unlike other antiques such as an eighteenth-century highboy or set of Windsor chairs, the odds of which turning up at a garage sale in Idaho or at a flea market in West Virginia are comparable to meeting the late Greta Garbo at a Burger King in Kalamazoo. The golden age of the country store in America was the 1880–1940 period. There were corner groceries and country stores in every city, hamlet, and semi-major crossroads in the United States. Urban and rural stores all contained similar signs, counters, cast-iron coffee grinders, and had products for sale that are eagerly sought after by collectors today. Rare pieces are found in attics, basements, at tag sales, and upscale antiques shows in New York City.

We have consistently found that dealers who specialize in a particular aspect of the antiques and collectibles field tend to have more realistic price structure than dealers who only occasionally have an item that falls within that category. A dealer who features advertising and country store items knows the marketplace, is aware of relative values, and tends to be realistic. A glass, stoneware, jewelry, or furniture dealer who acquires a collection and finds an isolated store or advertising piece often has to guess at the pricing. The tendency is to guess higher than the item's probable value.

There is a trend with individual collectors to specialize within the field of advertising and country store antiques. This has been a somewhat recent development because of escalating prices and a constantly dwindling supply of rarities. A piece of advertising that was labeled as "uncommon" six years ago would now probably be termed "rare." When pieces are inexpensive and available in quantity, mistakes and miscalculations mean relatively little. As an example, over the past twenty years Shaker seed boxes have increased from approximately $125 to $1,000 in value. It takes considerably more knowledge about an item to feel comfortable about its authenticity at $1,000 than at $125.

Condition is a critical factor in evaluating country store antiques. Unlike a piece of furniture that has undergone some minor restoration, a store fixture, tobacco tin, or paper sign that has been repaired, repainted, or had parts replaced is significantly diminished in value and desirability.

It is essential that, when making a carefully considered purchase for your collection, you secure a detailed receipt from the seller. The receipt should include:

The dealer's name, address, and telephone number.

The date of the purchase and a description of the item(s). The description should include a notation about any alterations or existing damage to the piece. These would include repainting, water spots, tears, etc.

If the dealer has a return policy or guarantee, it should be added to the receipt. Develop a filing system for your receipts and store them in a fireproof box.

The dealer's or seller's signature is an absolute must or the receipt has no meaning.

Sample Receipt 1 shows minimum information and should not be accepted by the buyer. Sample Receipt 2 contains all the information the buyer needs.

Payment by check guarantees you a backup receipt that is endorsed by the seller.

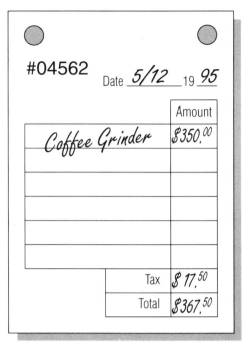

Sample receipt 1.

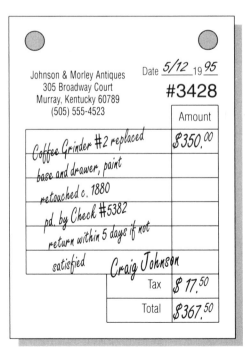

Sample receipt 2.

Shops

As you certainly know by now, the North American antiques shop is considered a seriously endangered species. Only a miniscule percentage of the surviving shops specialize in advertising and country store-related antiques and collectibles. We are somewhat optimistic that reports of the demise of the antiques shop may be premature. It appears to us that quality antiques shops will gradually reappear as collectors become increasingly disenchanted with the proliferation of "antiques" malls filled with crafts, reproductions, and last year's *Sports Illustrated* swimsuit issue.

A midwestern antiques shop that specializes in advertising and country store-related items is The General Store, located at 3431 State Rd., 26 East, Lafayette, Indiana 47905.

Auctions

Auctions can be an exceptional source of advertising and country store antiques when longtime collections are broken up by death, divorce, or disinterest. Many major American auction houses typically conduct auctions each year with profusely illustrated and detailed catalogues. The *Maine Antiques Digest, Antique Review* (formerly *Ohio Antique Review*), and *Antique Week* are the places to look for the announcement and advertisement of upcoming auction events.

Garth's Auctions of Delaware, Ohio, is one of the nation's best-known sources for Americana sold at auction. Garth's offers catalogues for each of their sales by mail and encourages telephone bidding. Information or a catalogue subscription can be secured by contacting Garth's Auctions Inc., 2690 Stratford Road, Box 369, Delaware, Ohio 43015, (614) 362-4771 (phone) or (614) 363-0164 (fax).

Buying at Auction

1. Attend the preview or show up the day of the auction an hour early to determine if everything is as advertised.

2. Decide on a price range for each item in which you have any interest. Regardless of how emotionally involved you become or incensed at a fellow bidder, do not exceed your limits.

3. Be assertive in the bidding process. Don't give the impression that your bid is tentative. You want the individual bidding against you to know that you are going to buy the item.

4. If your predetermined price limit is $300 for a cast-iron coffee grinder and the auctioneer is at $135 and slowing down, secure the victory by bidding $175.

5. A "shill" is someone whose reason for existing is to raise the bidding process with no intent to actually purchase or keep the item being sold. Sometimes the auctioneer has a shill (or two) in the audience. More often a friend or family member of the owner of the pieces being auctioned is there to make sure there are no bargains. If you maintain your predetermined highest bid level, you have paid approximately what you had in mind regardless of the shill's activities.

6. Find out before the auction begins if there is a buyer's premium. The buyer's premium is a charge of an additional 10–20% of the selling price of each item. For example, the $300 you bid for the coffee

grinder is actually going to result in a cost of $330 with the 10% buyer's premium.

7. When you get your bidding number prior to the start of the auction, find out the auctioneer's preferred method of payment and what the rules of the auction are. The serious auction goer will have already become familiar with the rules prior to day of the event by securing a sale bill or catalogue several days in advance.

8. Show up at the auction under the assumption that you are going to be buying something. If you are interested in a counter or display case, bring a truck or van. If your mission is to purchase primarily "smalls" (dishes, jewelry, books), bring boxes and packing materials.

9. It is the ultimate misconception to assume that prices will go "through the roof" if antiques dealers show up at the auction. The dealer or picker in attendance who makes a purchase must mark it up at least 35–50% to make a profit. A collector can pay retail value at an auction much more quickly than a dealer who is buying to resell.

10. If the auction is going to be held outside, assume that it will be absolutely the worst weather possible for that particular season. Make it a point to dress accordingly.

Finds

Several years ago a dealer at the 3rd Sunday Market in Bloomington, Illinois, offered for sale a dozen early twentieth-century folding chairs that he had purchased from a 100-year-old funeral home that was moving to a new facility. The chairs had been covered with sev-eral coats of fabric over the years and were in almost pristine condition after the cloth was removed. He had paid $10 each for the chairs and was hoping to roll each one over quickly into a twenty dollar bill.

When he removed the fabric from the first eleven chairs he found precisely what he expected. They were in good repair with a heavy varnished finish. The twelfth chair turned out to be something special.

In the early 1900s several tobacco manufacturers produced chairs that were made available to rural and small-town general and grocery stores for the locals to recline in and share their personal triumphs and tragedies on hot August afternoons or in February snowstorms around the potbellied stove and the checkerboard.

This particular chair had a courting scene painted on the front panel and an African-American wedding scene on the back panel. The new owner of the chair was well aware of its value and priced it accordingly. For the dealer it was unquestionably a "find" because he was going to make hundreds of dollars in profit on a $10 investment. It turned out to be a "find" for the serious collector who purchased it because it was a "fresh" piece that had not been offered before. A "find" by definition is something great, at a reasonable price, that surfaces when you least expect it. Country store antiques can be found almost everywhere because country stores were almost everywhere. We are absolutely convinced that there is at least one more "find" out there.

Flea Markets

The absolutely best aspect of most flea markets is the uncertainty of what you are going to find. There is still a thrill of anticipation for us even after 25 years of attending markets across the country. Once or twice a year we find something that wipes out the memory of being shut out on a 98° day in July.

Flea market promoters tend to allow their exhibitors to offer for sale almost anything that may legally be exchanged. We have sifted through Bobby Vee albums, bus tokens, and preworn underwear to find something of consequence. Attending a flea market is an emotional and physically debilitating experience that only periodically is rewarded with a meaningful purchase; but that one purchase usually makes all the wasted trips immediately worthwhile.

If you feel that the flea market may have something that you want, the key to success is to get inside the door during the setup period before the place can be "picked" by the participating dealers. Rent a space or pay the "early bird" ticket price, but make an effort to get into the market as early as possible.

Antiques Markets

Antiques markets are very attractive to dealers because they provide the potential for large crowds with a minimal investment in time and overhead expenses. There are primarily two distinct types of antiques markets in operation—multiple shows and one-time or annual shows. Many markets are held six, eight, or twelve times a year on a regular date (for example, the third Sunday or first weekend of the month) at a fairgrounds or facility with extensive parking and buildings for inside dealers. Typically, these markets are near a populated area with nearby interstate highways and are often heavily advertised, bringing dealers from several states. The alternative to multiple shows or markets is the prestigous one-

or two-day show often held annually to benefit a local charity or historical site.

If a comparison is to be made between the typical antiques market and flea market, the following statements are generally true:

Antiques markets tend to be monitored much more closely by the promoter for quality and authenticity than flea markets.

Country store collectors are much more likely to find a broader and more diverse selection of items from which to choose at an antiques market.

More dealers who specialize in advertising and country store antiques would be found at the antiques market.

The odds of discovering an underpriced "find" would be greater at a flea market.

The dealers at the antiques market tend to price their merchandise realistically because they buy and sell it on a daily basis.

Flea market dealers who only periodically encounter advertising and country store antiques tend to price their merchandise at extremes.

Antiques market dealers tend to scout or "pick" the show prior to its opening much more closely than flea market dealers.

Specialty Shows

As the interest in country store antiques continues to evolve, there will be an increased number of antiques shows devoted exclusively to advertising. The "original" advertising and country store show is held three times each year in Indianapolis, Indiana, at the Indiana State Fairgrounds on 38th Street. The show is promoted by Kim and Mary Kokles, P.O. Box 475092, Garland, TX 75047.

Price Trends

In 1967 Ernest L. Pettit wrote *The Book of Collectible Tin Containers with Price Guide.* Mr. Pettit's book was one of the very early attempts to provide information and values for advertising and country store antiques. In the Introduction to the book he states:

Collecting old tins for a hobby can be a lot of fun and very interesting. Many of the companies which manufactured the products these old tins once contained are no longer in existence. Others were long ago sold to companies which are today popular manufacturing companies.

When the collector goes out to purchase old tins, he will find that the prices vary greatly. The cost will depend upon three things: where he finds them, how old they are, and their condition. Antique dealers set their own individual prices. These prices reflect how much they had to pay for them, and how scarce they think the tins may be. I have paid as little as twenty-five cents, and as much as thirty-five dollars for some of those that I have in my own collection, which includes tins for tobacco, medicines, chemicals, powders, foodstuffs, and many more too numerous to mention at this time.

To gain some perspective on current prices for tins, let's compare Mr. Pettit's 1967 values with an estimated value for a comparable tin today. Assume that all of the tins are in at least "excellent" condition.

Description of Tin	1967 Value	1995 Value
Huntley & Palmer Biscuits, made in the shape of a stack of books with a brown "leather" type strap binding the books, hinged lid.	$40–$60	$150–$200
Tiger Chewing Tobacco, 11″ high, cylindrical in form, hinged lid, P. Lorillard & Co. (red).	$8–$12	$100–$150
Just Suits Tobacco, hinged lid, lunchbox type, 8″ × 5″ × 4″.	$3–$5	$125–$140
Union Leader Tobacco, hinged lid, lunchbox type, 8″ × 5″ × 4″.	$3–$5	$65–$75
Central Union Cut Plug Tobacco, hinged lid, lunchbox type.	$6–$8	$115–$130
Mayo's Brownie, pull-off lid, Humpty-Dumpty (roly-poly) type, Mayo Tobacco Co., "the Storekeeper."	$7–$15	$450–$575
Famous Cake Box Mixture, 5″ × 4″ × 3¼″, hinged lid, Leavitt & Peirce.	$3–$5	$50–$60
Planter's Peanuts, cylindrical form, 9½″ × 26½″, pull-off lid.	$5–$8	$135–$150
Cough Cherries, pull-off lid, D.G. Stoughton.	$3–$5	$175–$200
Bagley's Wild Fruit Tobacco, lunchbox type, John J. Bagley & Co.	$4–$7	$135–$150

Resources

Ephemera Society, 124 Elm St., Bennington, VT 05201.

National Association of Paper and Advertising Collectors, P.O. Box 471, Columbia, PA 17512.

Tin Container Collectors' Association (T.C.C.A.), Box 440101, Aurora, CO 80044. Founded in 1971 with 35 collectors, the T.C.C.A. is now an international organization with 3,000 members. The *Tintype*, a bimonthly newsletter, has a "buy and sell" section, a history of various tin containers, and estimates of their degree of relative rarity.

Tuckaway General Store and Apothecary Shop, Shelburne Museum, Shelburne, VT 05482. The Shelburne Museum is one of those places you visit because you want to and not merely because you are passing by or are in the immediate area. It is located in northwestern Vermont and houses one of the nation's premiere Americana collections. The Shelburne's spacious grounds are not inundated with visitors on the busiest day of the year. The atmosphere is relaxed and there are buildings filled with collections that satisfy every collector's needs from circus to Shaker items. The Tuckaway General Store and Apothecary Shop is itself worth the trip up Route 7.

Roselyn Grossholz's *Country Store Collectibles* (Wallace-Homestead Book Co., 1972) was probably the first book written on the subject. Long out of print, it is a lavishly illustrated volume that contains a price list that dramatizes how values have evolved over the past two decades. If you ever have the opportunity to buy the book, do so. You'll enjoy it.

The Antique Review (Worthington, Ohio) and the *Maine Antiques Digest* (Waldoboro, Maine) provide exceptional coverage of major auctions and shows involving advertising and country store antiques. The articles are usually loaded with pictures and prices.

Interview with Chris Fricker

Chris Fricker, a respected midwestern auctioneer, is becoming well known for his country store and advertising auctions. He is in constant contact with buyers and sellers. His comments are especially valuable in an environment of rising prices and a falling supply of quality items. You may contact him at P.O. Box 852, Bloomington, IL 61702.

Q. If you were going to start collecting advertising/country store antiques in this market, what would you buy?

A. I would look for one-pound "screw on" or "slip on" coffee tins. I honestly don't believe that collectors realize how difficult examples in good condition have become to find.

Q. What category of country store/advertising pieces do you feel are underpriced today?

A. Spice tins and sample tins are seriously underpriced presently. Sample tins are miniature versions that were provided to customers trying out the product.

Q. What items are overpriced?

A. My view may be a little jaded because I collect them, but I feel that peanut butter pails are overpriced.

Q. Where is the best place to look for country store antiques?

A. The Indianapolis Advertising Show is a primary source for collectors in middle America. I also look for pieces at antiques markets and flea markets because you never know for sure what is going to turn up.

Q. Are reproductions a problem for collectors of country store/advertising material?

A. Reproductions of advertising are beginning to kill a great hobby. They are of special concern to new buyers and collectors who have not seen enough old items to have a standard of comparison. In the past four or five years there have been numerous attempts to reproduce a variety of tin and paper signs.

PART TWO

Picture Price Guide

The surviving country stores we have encountered appear at first glance to be somewhat haphazardly put together. A closer inspection reveals a pattern of organization that leads the customer through the store in a meaningful manner. Our intention for organizing the price section of this book was to take the reader along a similar path.

The items that follow were commonly available in country stores during the second half of the nineteenth century (1850–1900):

baked goods
baskets
beer and whiskey
brooms and brushes
candles
candy
caskets
cider
clocks and watches
clothing
coffee and tea
dishes
graniteware
groceries
hardware
locally grown fruits and vegetables

lumber

meat

medicines and miracle cures

musical instruments

milk and cheese

oysters

sewing supplies

shoes and boots

spices

sporting goods

stoneware

stoves

string and rope

tinware

tools

toys

woodenware

A large "crossover" category for collecting is advertising. Collectors of advertising are constantly searching for every aspect of the country store from the screened front door to signs, coffee grinders, shelving, and chopping blocks. As shown in the list above, anything that was part of the store, hauled to the store, or sold in the store is highly collectible.

Seed Boxes

The Shakers are given credit for developing the idea of marketing individual packet of garden seeds rather than selling seed by the scoop from a barrel or by the pound. The Shakers provided stores with counter display boxes that contained descriptive and colorful interior and exterior paper labels and seed packets. At the conclusion of the marketing season representatives of the Shakers would return to the stores, settle up with the owners, retrieve the boxes and pick up any unsold packets. The boxes would be relabeled over the winter months and redistributed and stocked with fresh seeds in the early spring.

Other seed growers immediately saw the success and profit the Shakers were enjoying from their innovative marketing approach and produced their own seed boxes and individual packets of garden and vegetable seeds.

The earliest seed boxes date from the mid-nineteenth century.

Notes on Collecting Seed Boxes

1. The most desirable seed boxes contain a colorful interior and exterior label, the original finish on the box, the original hinges (leather, wire, or metal), and the interior partitions (dividers) used to separate the seed packets.

2. The typical late nineteenth- and early twentieth-century seed boxes measure approximately 20″–24″ wide × 10″–12″ deep × 4″–6″ high.

3. Paper labels tend to dry out over time. Very few boxes are found with the original labels in pristine condition. Expect some damage to the labels but look for boxes with *both* labels.

4. The earliest seed boxes were made of soft woods (pine or poplar). Smaller boxes of oak were products of the twentieth century when counter display area was much more limited.

5. Many seed companies kept the same boxes and glued new labels on top of one another each year. It is possible that a better label is hiding under the one that appears to be heavily damaged.

6. Some seed companies bought stock or standard labels and had their local name printed on the stock label. You may find a box from Maine and another example from Indiana with the same labels.

7. If a box is going to be missing a label, it is an excellent bet that it will be the exterior label. Interior labels were protected when the lids were closed and the boxes stored.

8. Rarely will a seed box be found that was handcrafted rather than factory-made. Most of the boxes have machine dovetails or are nailed (round heads) at the corners.

9. Based on their degree of rarity, we are convinced that seed boxes with their colorful and original interior and exterior labels are seriously underpriced at $200–$300 each.

10. Other than Shaker brand seed boxes, the individual company is of little consequence in determining value. Keep in mind that when you pay $300 for a seed box you are buying two labels (worth $250) and a $50 (at most) wooden box. Without the labels the seed box has minimal value.

Rare Shaker seed box from Mt. Lebanon, N.Y., with interior and exterior labels. **$3500–$4500**

Stickney and Poor's Mustard box. **$150–$160**

E. B. Millar & Co. Penang Spice box. **100–$125**

Hiram Sibley & Co. seed box with original seed bundles and packets. **$1100–$1300**

Stickney and Poor's Mustard box. $175–$225

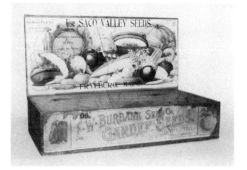

E. W. Burbank Garden Seeds display box, Dated 1906. $300–$335

Reliable Seeds counter display box. $200–$240

Shaker's Garden Seeds box. $1200–$1500

Shakers Genuine Garden Seeds box. $1100–$1300

Rice's Seeds box. $300–$335

Rice's Seeds box with less colorful label. $275–$325

Briggs Brothers seed box. **$300–$335**

Thos. W. Emerson & Co. Northern Grown Seeds display box. **$225–$275**

Budd D. Hawkins Northern Seeds display box. **$300–$335**

Button's Raven Gloss Shoe Dressing box. **$135–$165**

Stickney and Poor's Mustard box without a top. **$60–$70**

Lewis Atwood & Son Seeds display box. **$400–$450**

R. Durkee & Co. spices box. **$100–$125**

Hiram Sibley & Co. Seeds display box. $350–$385

Somerset Garden Seeds display box, c. mid-nineteenth century. $350–$400

Philips Choice Vegetable Seeds box. $325–$350

Catalogue (interior label) of Somerset box showing contents.

White Fawn Biscuit box. $125–$140

Rice's seed box, oak, early twentieth century.
$100–$125

Sioux City Seed Co. tomato seed packet.
$9–$11

Metal display rack for packets of garden seeds, complete with original decorative decals. $700–$900

Sioux City Seed Co. beet seed packet. $9–$11

Rare Shaker's Seeds box with colorful exterior label. $1500–$1800

Cressler's Wild Rose Tooth Powder counter display box with unopened containers. $275–$300

Interior label of Shaker seed box showing contents.

Shakers Garden Seeds box, c. 1861. $1200–$1400

William Burt pea seed box. $6–$8

1912 Seed Book from Fairview Seed Farms.
$25–$30

Betsy Ross Shoe Polish with original un-opened contents. $235–$300

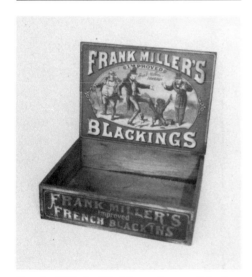

Frank Miller's Blackings shoe polish box.
$200–$250

Sioux City Seed Co. squash seed packet.
$8–$10

Lid from a Dixie Chews molasses candy box with colorful interior label. **$150–$200**

Hirdoo Brand Spices box. **$100–$125**

Northrup King & Co. seed calendar from 1922. **$85–$100**

Painted pine store box for seed samples, c. late nineteenth century. **$350–$400**

Red Ranger cigar box for counter sales. **$65–$85**

Glass jars for storing beet and kale seeds from twentieth-century hardware store. $20–$25 each

Glass seed jars, twentieth century. $20–$25 each

Seed storage jars with pouring lids, c. 1940s. $35–$50 each

Tango Stogies tin. $55–$65

Silver Cream silver polish box. $40–$45

Turned wooden Carter's Blue Black Fountain Pen Ink container. $50–$55

Turned wooden Carter's Fountain Pen Fluid container. $50–$55

Finck's Overalls paper stand-up. $65–$75

Sawyer Biscuit Company animal cracker box.
$25–$28

Velvetina Face Powder box. $20–$25

Utica Sport Coat box. $24–$28

Velvetina Talcum container. $35–$40

Box and bottle of Carter's Indelible Ink.
$40–$45

Cast zinc trade sign clock from a jewelry store, c. 1900. **$400–$575**

Uncle John's Syrup stand-up with rare cane and maple sugar syrup can. **$250–$300**

Partridge Pure Lard can. **$40–$45**

Blue Diamond almond stand-up. **$75– $100**

Betsy Ross Shoe Polish cans. **$25–$35 each**

Fleck's Hoof Packing box. $35–$50

Corticelli Spool Silk box and contents. $30–$35

Dr. Drake's Croup stand-up. $225–$250

Big Smith Shirt cardboard stand-up. $65–$75

Buster Brown Mustard can. $85–$110

Miller's Lasting Starch box. $30–$50

Dr. Caldwell Syrup Pepsin stand-up.
$300–$375

Hoosier Poet Mustard Seed can. $100–$150

Setsnug Underwear box. $75–$85

Smith Brothers Cough Syrup box and unopened bottle. $65–$80

Kendall Soapine "The Dirt Killer" box. $65–$75

Black Cat Hosiery stand-up. $75–$85

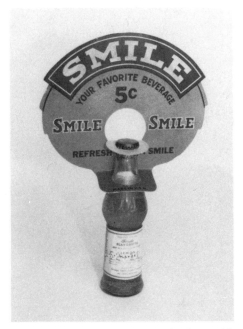

Smile soft drink counter display with unopened bottle. $75–$95

Red Kap Work Shirts box. *$50–$65*

Post Toasties Corn Flakes box. *$35–$50*

F.B. Gates grocery sack. *$4–$5*

Rare unopened box of Wrigley's Spearmint. *$450–$550*

Individual package of Wrigley's Spearmint. *$25–$35*

Wrigley's Chewing Gum counter display with packages. **$125–$150**

Cracker Jack box. **$65–$70**

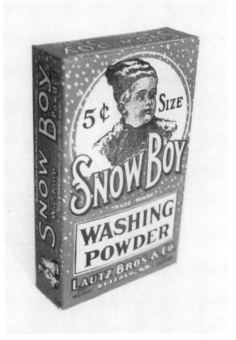

Snow Boy Washing Powder box. **$50–$60**

Shredded Wheat box. $60–$65

Kitchen Klenzer can. $35–$40

Back side of Shredded Wheat box.

Peacock Coffee container. $65–$70

Golden Robin cinnamon container. $15–$20

Quail Rolled Oats box. **$75–$85**

Robin ginger container. **$20–$25**

Morning Joy Tea container. **$35–$40**

Robin Tea container. **$40–$45**

Gold Medal Hosiery stand-up. **$125–$150**

Rare Underwood Talmage Co. candy tub or bucket. $600–$800

Board of Trade Fine Cut tobacco display container. $500–$700

Maytag Company oil can with pouring spout. $135–$150

Quaker Hominy Grits container. $40–$45

Fairy Soap oversized advertising box.
$150–$175

Pair of shoes, c. 1890-1900. **$65–$70**

Birdseye Sorghum can. **$30–$35**

Butterfinger candy bar box. **$75–$100**

Star Brand Shoes bench. **$500–$600**

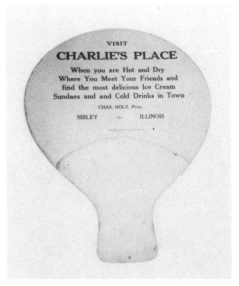

Advertising fan from Charlie's Place, Sibley, Ill. $15–$20

Back side of fan.

Bars of Lifebuoy and Swan soap. $10–$12 each

Rawleigh's cinnamon container. $25–$30

"Free" Dill's Best pipe cleaners counter display. $30–$35

Shaker Pickles bottle with original lid wrapper and lid. $500–$600

Shaker horse radish bottle. $300–$400

Candy tin from Bloomington, Illinois, made to resemble a workman's lunch pail, c. 1930. **$150–$175**

Grape-Nuts tin from the first quarter of the twentieth century. **$150–$200**

None-Such peanut butter pail. **$325–$400**

Tin Putnam dye cabinet. **$100–$150**

Fresh Roasted Coffee bag. **$10**

Star Bright Coffee bag. **$10**

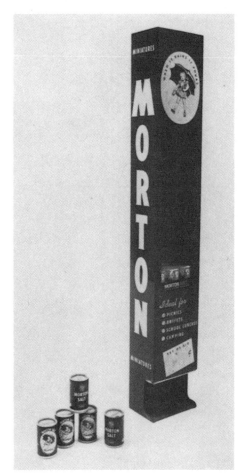

Morton Salt display. $150–$185

Sellers kitchen cabinet cooking chart.
$50–$60

Electrocuter electric mousetraps. $25 each

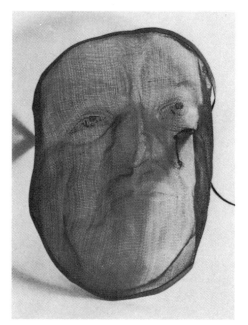

Loyal Order of the Red Men mesh mask.
$150–$175

Health Club baking powder grocer's "Want Book." $14–$16

Happy Bunny egg dye: each package, $6; display box, $50–$60

Wooden turnip kraut cutter. $150–$175

Girl clothes hanger made of heavy cardboard. $150–$175

Baby Ruth chewing gum. *$15–$20*

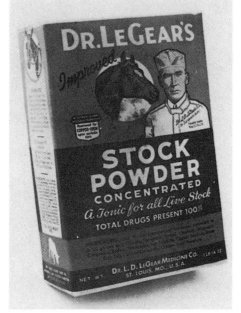

Dr. LeGear's stock powder. *$15*

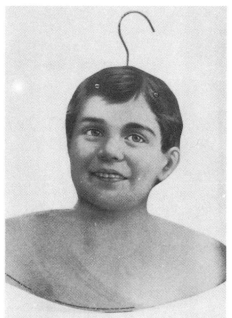

Boy clothes hanger made of heavy card-board. *$150–$175*

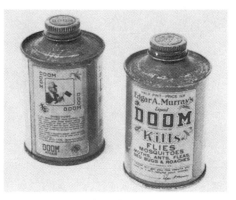

Doom bug killer. *$22–$25*

Egg-O Baking Powder can. $45–$55

Old Dutch can. $25–$30

Calf brains container. $25–$30

Breakfast Call Coffee tin. $55–$65

Can of Roast Mutton. $25–$35

Peter Rabbit peanut butter pail (back).
$500–$650

Richelieu coffee tin, three-pound size.
$75–$95

Hoffmann's Old Time coffee tin. $75–85

Ferndell coffee grinder. $235–$300

American Home Coffee container. $65– $75

Mirex cigar tin. $40–$50

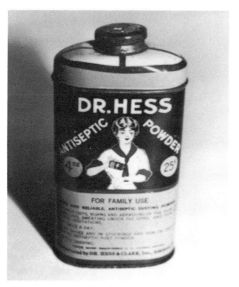

Dr. Hess tin. $12–$20

Advo Gold Medal Coffee tin. $65–$75

Program from Buffalo Bill's Wild West Show. $225–$275

P.O.C. Beer paper sign. $25–$35

Planters Mr. Peanut advertising: mug, $55–$60; salt and pepper, $200–$225; ashtray, $100–$125

Three paper toys: black child, $100–$125; monkey, $65–$75; cowboy, $50–$65

Coca-Cola Trays

1897–1902	Only round trays were made
1903–1910	Oval trays and round trays were made
1910–1921	Only oval and rectangular trays were made
After 1921	Only rectangular trays were made

Change or Tip Trays Made Between 1900 and 1920

| 1900–1906 | Round trays |
| 1907–1920 | Oval trays |

It is not unusual to find a change or tip tray in heavily used condition because most became ashtrays or coasters and suffered the consequences over the years. Rarely is a change or tip tray in pristine condition discovered.

Coca-Cola tray, 1948. $175–$200

Coca-Cola tray, 1920. $550–$625

Coca-Cola tray, 1938. $225–$275

Coca-Cola tray, 1950. *$85–$115*

Coca-Cola trays, from top left: 1917, $275–$325; 1914, $400–$500; 1920, $375–575

Coca-Cola trays, clockwise from top left: 1912, $400–$500; 1909, $450–$600; 1904, $500–$700

Coca-Cola thermometer, 1942. $325–$450

Coca-Cola thermometers, from left: 1936,
$250–$300; *1950,* ***$100–$125;*** *1939,*
$200–$250

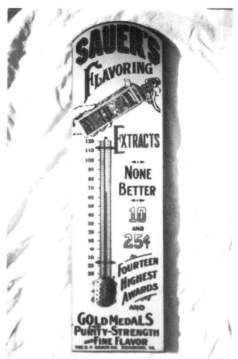

Sauer's Flavoring thermometer, c. 1918.
$650–$900

Coca-Cola thermometer, c. 1915. ***$750– $850***

Hills Brothers Coffee thermometer, c. 1920s.
$650–$800

$1000 Guaranteed bedbug killer. $30–$40

Blue Ribbon baking powder (in Ball canning jar, Muncie, Indiana). $20–$25

Topsy whitewash brush, "Set in Bakelite." $10–$15

Aer-Aid, "Absorbs Refrigerator Odors." $15–$20

Northern Seeds counter display box. $275–$300

Landers, Frary, and Clark coffee grinder.
$400–$500

Elgin National coffee mill, counter model.
$450–$650

Painted Apricot bucket, early 1900s.
$150–$175

Painted Plum bucket, early 1900s.
$250–$275

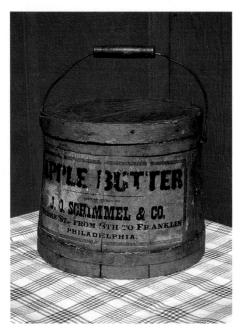

Painted Apple Butter bucket, early 1900s.
$150–$175

Preserves container with "drop" handle, c.
1920. $125–$140

Cyclone wheelbarrow, Louisville, Kentucky, c. 1920. **$210–$250**

Ex-Lax thermometer, c. 1930s. **$125–$150**

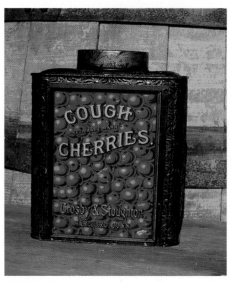

Cough Cherries cannister with removable label, used for counter sales. **$175–$200**

Bartlett pears cans, c. 1930s. **$12–$15 each**

Stoneware jug given as premium by local grocery store, Altoona, Pennsylvania. **$100–$125**

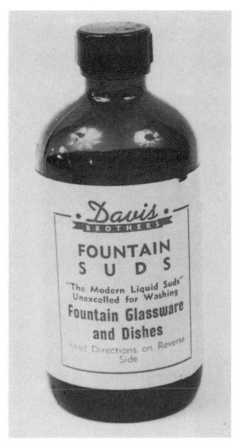

Davis Brothers Fountain Suds. $20–$25

Rub-No-More cleanser. $30–$40

Epsom salts tin. $125–$150

Butterfly Tints. $7–$10

Yourex Silver Saver. $55–$65

Octagon white toilet soap. $6–$8

Klex pumice soap. $8–$10

Heinz tomato ketchup store display bottle (was always empty). $75–$85

Victory chicken boxes, c. 1940s. **$20–$25 each**

Good Luck Jar Rubbers. **$20–$25**

Crow's Dependable Hybrid Seed Corn sack. **$20–$25**

Deck of playing cards, mid-nineteenth century. **$65–$85**

Stoneware rolling pins with maple handles, given as premiums by local grocery stores, early 1900s. $325–$385 each

Badger Matches. $12–$15

Bars of laundry soap: Big Jack, $6–$8; Blue Barrel, $5–$7

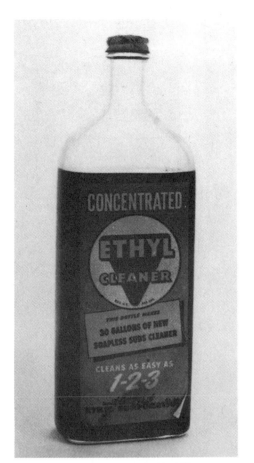

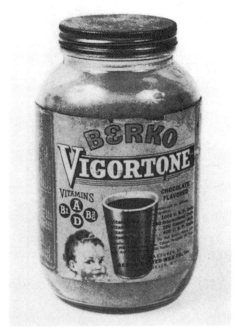

Berko Vigortone. $7–$10

Ethyl cleaner, concentrated. $9–$12

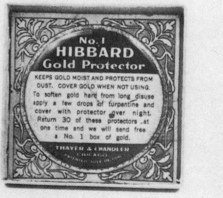

Thayer and Chandler Hibbard's Roman Gold. $15–$20

Fine Feathers Hosiery advertisement.
$20–$25

Preserve jar labels. $9–$12

La Dore's Bust Food. $100–$125

Wilknit hosiery samples. $20–$25

Wizard Dri-Cube (dry ice). $8–$12

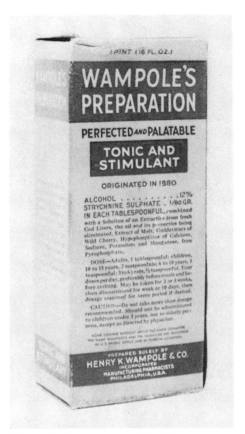

Wampole's Preparation. $20–$25

"Super Market Coloring Contest" book (advertises name-brand products). $20–$25

Wooden Johnson & Johnson display (Red Cross). $75–$100

Snow Crop advertising bear. **$225–$250**

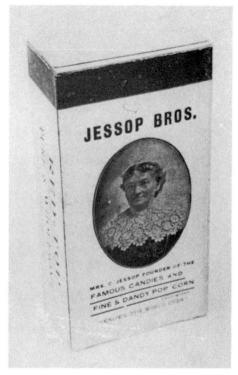

Jessop Bros. popcorn box. **$10–$15**

Dr. A. W. Chase's catarrh powder. **$12–$15**

Box from Snow Crop Quick Frozen Waffles. **$20–$22**

Hamburg Breast Tea. **$20–$25**

R and R Carbolized Mutton Tallow tin, free sample. $15–$20

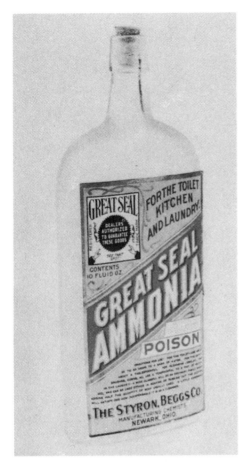

Great Seal ammonia bottle. $15–$20

Spurlock's Southern Laundry Washing Blue. $15–$20

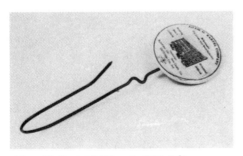

Adam H. Bartel bill hook. $55–$60

Virgin olive oil tin. $75–$100

Mallard prepared mustard jar. $35–$45

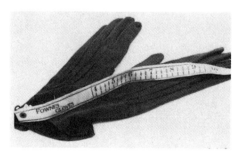

Fownes Gloves: gloves, $12–$15; glove measure, *$15–$20*

Ladies' high-top shoes, brown and black. $135–$150

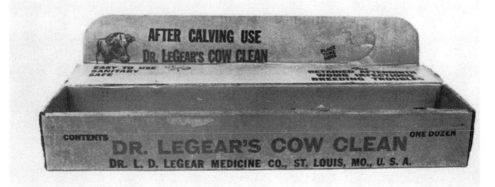

Dr. LeGear's Cow Clean: each tube, $20; extra sets of instructions, $3.50; display box, $75

Medical assortment, 666 brand: cold tablets (12 tablets), $7; cold preparation with quinine (4 oz.), $8.50; cold preparation (6 oz.), $10; cold capsules (36 tablets), $9.50

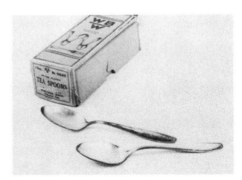

WB/W teaspoons (3 dozen). $45–$55

Smith Brothers' cough syrup. $15–$20

Hansdown hand cleaner. $25–$30

666 display box. $175–$200

666 display box plus items. $175–$200

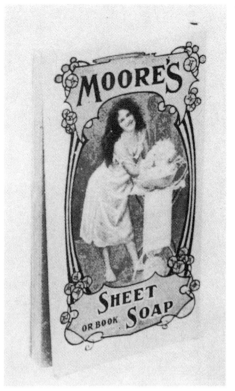

Moore's sheet soap book. $30–$35

Renner floating coffee cooker. $20–$25

Quaker Oats crayons. $15–$20

Purity sheet soap book. $25–$30

Papier-mâché milk bottle, "Order a Quart of Delicious Chocolate Flavored Milk" (store display). $50–$75

Christmas cigarette house, Camel. $15–$20

Christmas cigarette house, Salem. $15–$20

Domes of Silence (casters). $15–$20

Sergeant's Skip-Stain (used to prevent pet stains). $10–$12

George F. Cram marking pencils. $8–$10

Cardinal Meteor flints and wicks. $16

Canada Dry quinine water. $12–$14

Chi-namel furniture polish. $15

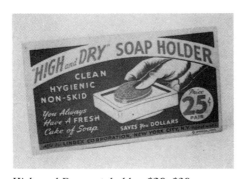

High and Dry soap holder. $20–$30

Empress Hosiery box. $20–$30

Putnam's Bath Bloom display box (4 packages). $10–$15

Putnam's Bath Bloom, package only. $5

Innerclean Herbal Laxative. $10–$15

Wright's liquid smoke. $10–$15

Chinaman laundry bag. $45–$55

Navon Complete Book-keeping System.
$15–$20

Gem City Ice Cream sign (chocolate marsh-mallow). $45–$55

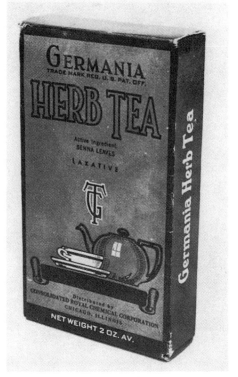

Germania herb tea. $10–$12

St. Joseph Aspirin clock. $130–$150

Fru-Tola dispenser. $400–$500

Baker's glass store jar. $100–$125

National Biscuit Company wood and glass display case. $425–$525

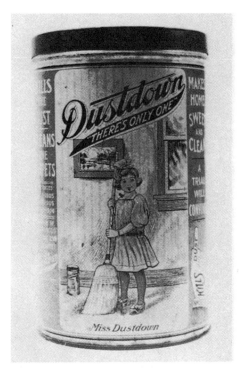

Dustdown tin. *$95–$110*

Maroc baby powder tin. *$20–$25*

"Frogletts" tin (Durante's Cough Tablets):
"A Froglett a Day Keeps Your Cough Away."
$160–$175

Cupid Chaser. *$40–$50*

Syrup of Figs and Elixir of Senna (California Fig Syrup Co.), free sample. **$50–$75**

Regoes rubbed sage tin. **$15–$20**

Cardboard advertising display for Spry shortening. **$100–$125**

Seaco tin thread holder. **$70–$75**

Tim's Cap box. $100–$125

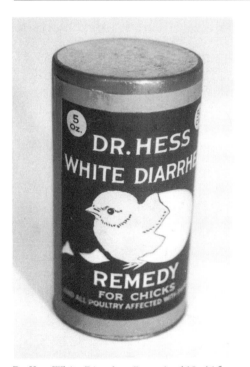

Dr. Hess White Diarrhea Remedy. $12–$16

College Girl Tea container. $28–$32

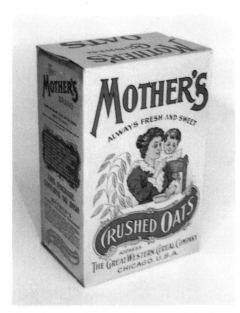

Box of Mother's Crushed Oats. $35–$45

Tender and Tasty Popped Corn box. $30–$40

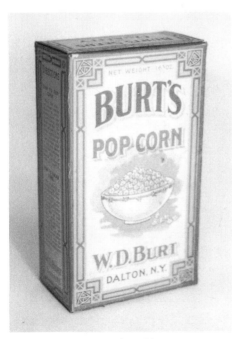

Burt's Pop Corn box. $30–$40

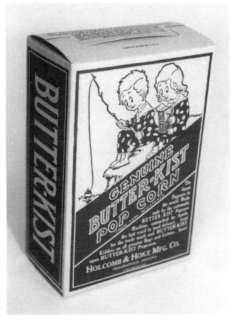

Butter-Kist popcorn box. $30–$40

Holstein Bell No. 3. **$75–$85**

Campbell Brand Coffee can. **$40–$60**

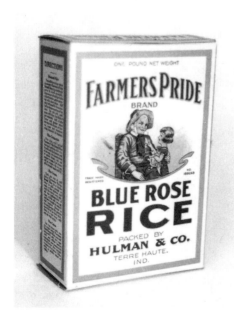

Blue Rose Rice box. **$12–$16**

Tomson's Red Seal Cleanser. **$20–$30**

Dyanshine Stove Polish. $10–$12

ABC cards. $9–$11

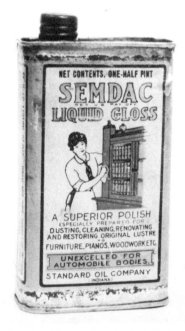

Semdac Liquid Gloss polish. $15–$18

Clean Wall Cleaner. $10–$15

Wet-Me-Wet glass and silver cleaner. $7–$9

Mocha-Java Coffee can. $45–$55

Superior Pickles bottle with original paper labels. $100–$125

Fresh Grand Chum Salmon cans. $15–$20 each

Fairbank's Gold Dust washing powder box. $40–$50

Late nineteenth-century Sugar Corn can.
$75–$85

LaCreole Hair Dressing bottle. $50–$75

Black Beauty Axle Grease can. $50–$55

Rich's Famous Julia Marlowe Shoes box.
$30–$50

The Pussy Cat Ten Pins game. **$150–$175**

Royal Baking Powder price plaque. **$75–$85**

Thomson and Taylor Space Co. coffee bin. **$325–$450**

1920s valentine. **$15–$20**

Box of stick cinnamon. **$8–$10**

Brown's French Dressing box. **$15–$18**

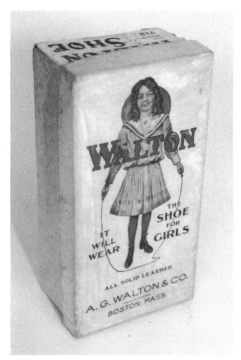

Walton Shoe box. **$50–$60**

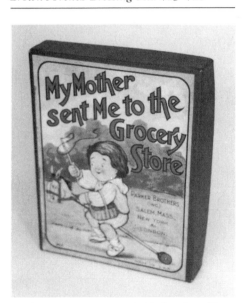

Parker Brothers game, My Mother Sent Me to the Grocery Store. **$100–$120**

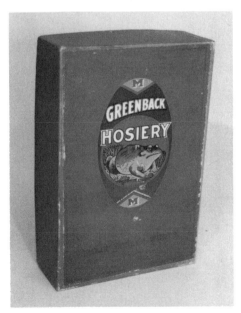

Greenback Hosiery box. **$35–$50**

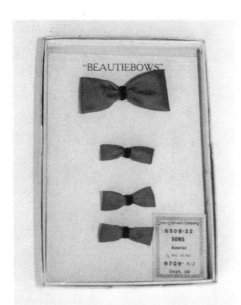

Beautiebows display. $50–$75

Kentucky Cardinal Hosiery box. $35–$55

Fairbank's Gold Dust Washing Powder case.
$100–$125

Three-bar box of Woodbury's Facial Soap.
$20–$25

Gilliam's Blue Grass Candies box. $35–$55

Shoelace counter display. $75–$85

Sharples Cream Separators sign. *$200–$225*

Tic-Toc dishwashing powder. *$8–$12*

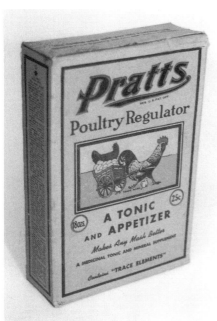

Bull Dog Liquid Spray Insecticide. *$18– $24*

Pratts Poultry Regulator tonic. *$20–$25*

Butler Brothers 1920 catalog. **$30–$40**

D. Crawford's New Store advertising stand-up c. 1905. **$200–$250**

Demon Lunch 5¢ candy bar box. **$75–$100**

"Merry Christmas, Happy New Year" box, c. 1910. **$150–$175**

Wooden milk box, "Return to Walker Gordon."
$130–$160

Duck Bones tin. **$85–$100**

Bean-X (strings green beans), c. WW II.
$20–$25

Nordmann's Original canned pumpernickel bread tin. **$10–$15**

Jar of crushed peach, The Cincinnati Extract Works. **$50–$60**

Breakstone's Pop Corn Style creamed cottage cheese tin. $40–$50

Hoosier Club coffee tin. $165–$185

Purina Dog Chow sample. $25–$35

Quaker Oats price marker. $20–$30

Calumet baking powder tin. $10–$15

Lemon wafer tin. $15–$20

Old Label baking powder container. $15–$25

Old Judge coffee container. $35–$50

Sir Walter Raleigh smoking tobacco container. $20–$25

Burnham Bartlett pears tin can. $12–$15

Edgeworth tobacco tin (pocket). $20–$30

Violet Bartlett pears. $12–$15

Krak-R-Jak Biscuits container. $30–$45

Jolly Time Pop Corn tin. $50–$75

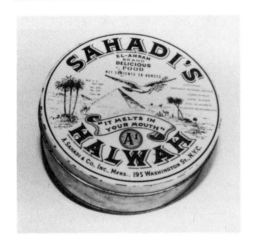

Sahadi's Halwah circular tin. $25–$35

Queen's Taste coffee tin. **$50–$60**

Ezra Williams flower seeds box. **$325– $375**

Mason's shoe polish box with paper labels. **$135–$150**

Coca-Cola tray, early 1920s. **$375–$575**

Stickney & Poor's Mustard box. **$175–$225**

Cast-Iron Coffee Mills

When a cast-iron coffee mill is evaluated, it is critical that the following elements be considered:

Paint. If the mill has been repainted, heavily "touched up," or the paint is seriously worn, the value of the piece is significantly diminished. Typically, the paint has faded and is not as robust as the day it was brought into the store, and that is expected by collectors today.

Original wooden drawer. Drawers have a tendency to fall out or be misplaced over the years. The original drawer should show wear from daily use over many years. It is a plus if the decal showing the size of the mill is still on the drawer front.

Base. Many of the mills had a soft wood base.

Stenciling. Like the paint, the original stenciled decoration should still be on the mill.

Decals. The decals are less important than the overall quality of the painted finish, but should be still on the mill.

Eagle dome top or finial. It is becoming unusual to find a mill that has an intact eagle finial or dome top. Most were lost or had the wings or heads broken off at some point.

Most collectors are interested in the smaller mills that are functional and even use them to grind coffee. The larger Enterprise mills can weigh over 200 pounds and are less desirable because of their unwieldy size. The illustration of mills that follow were part of the 1886 catalogue of the Enterprise Manufacturing Company of Philadelphia, Pennsylvania.

American Coffee, Spice and Drug Mill.

No. 1, with Iron Hopper holding 4 ounces Coffee.

SHOWING Nº I MILL CLOSED.

SHOWING Nº I. MILL OPEN.

THE above cuts represent our smallest Counter Mill, both closed and open, and illustrate the simple principle of operating our Mills, and the easy mode of opening them. It stands 12½ inches high, weighs 8 pounds, grinds 6 ounces of Coffee per minute and is regulated to grind coarse or fine by a thumb-screw on the side. It is adapted to family use and prescription counters.

PRICE,   .   .   . $2.00.

American Coffee, Spice and Drug Mill.

No. 2, RED. No. 102, MAROON.   No. 2½, RED. No. 102½, MAROON.

OUR Nos. 2 and 2½ Mills are alike, excepting as to dome, and will grind 6 ounces of Coffee per minute. They are very desirable for prescription counters and family use.

Iron Hopper; holding 4 ounces
Coffee stands 10½ inches high,
and weighs 11 pounds.

Nickel-plated Hopper, holding 7 ounces
Coffee, stands 15 in. high, and weighs 10 lbs

PRICE, $3.00.

PRICE, $4.00.

Extra Grinders, for Nos.	1, 2, 2½, 3, 4,	. . . .	Per Pair,	$ .75
" "	" 5, 6, 7, 8,	. . . .	" "	1.00
" "	" 9 to 18,	. . . .	" "	2.00
" "	" 18½ to 20	. . . .	" "	3.00

GRINDERS WARRANTED EQUAL TO STEEL.

American Coffee, Spice and Drug Mill.

No. 3, RED. No. 103, MAROON.

With Iron Hopper holding ½ pound of Coffee.

THIS Mill is 15 inches high, weighs 19 pounds, grinds one-half pound of Coffee per minute, has two 10-inch fly-wheels, and is very suitable for prescription counters, hotels, boarding houses, etc.

PRICE, . . . $5.00.

American Coffee, Spice and Drug Mill.

No. 4, RED. No. 104, MAROON.

NICKEL-PLATED Hopper and Eagle Dome Top, holding one pound of Coffee, stands 20½ inches high, weighs 18½ pounds, has two 10-inch fly-wheels, and will grind one-half pound of Coffee per minute.

PRICE, . . . $8.00.

GRINDERS WARRANTED EQUAL TO STEEL.

American Coffee, Spice and Drug Mill.

No. 9, RED. No. 109, MAROON.

With Iron Hopper holding 3 pounds Coffee.

SHOWING MILL CLOSED.

THIS is one of our most popular Counter Mills. It stands 24 inches high, weighs 80 pounds; has two 20-inch fly-wheels, and grinds two pounds of Coffee per minute. It is a very suitable size for grinding drugs and spices, for which purpose we furnish extra-fine grinders when so ordered.

THE principle upon which all our American Coffee, Spice and Drug Mills operate, the easy mode of opening them and the facility with which the interior parts may be got at or taken out for cleaning, etc., are apparent from the annexed engraving.

SHOWING MILL OPEN.

PRICE, $16.00.   Pulleys for Steam-power, $6.00 extra.

GRINDERS WARRANTED EQUAL TO STEEL.

American Coffee, Spice and Drug Mill.

No. 10, RED.   No. 110, MAROON.

Nickel-plated Hopper and Eagle Dome Top holding
6 pounds Coffee.

STANDS two feet four inches high, weighs 75 pounds, has two 20-inch fly-wheels, grinds two pounds of Coffee per minute.   A fine wooden drawer in the base receives the article ground.   This is a very handsome Counter Mill.   The grinders are made of hard, chilled iron and are warranted as durable as steel.

PRICE, $23.00.   Pulleys for Steam-power, $6.00, extra.

American Coffee, Spice and Drug Mill.

No. 18½,   **No. 118½,**

COLOR, VERMILION and GOLD.   **COLOR, MAROON and GOLD.**

Nickel-plated Hopper and Eagle Dome Top holding 10 lbs. Coffee

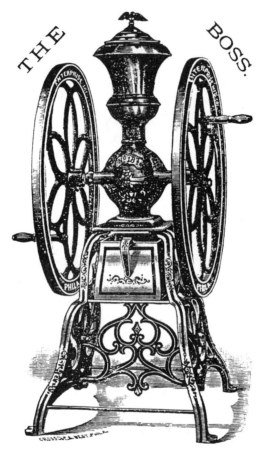

THIS is our favorite Mill. It well deserves the title of "The Boss," being without doubt the finest working and most rapid grinding Mill ever made. It is five feet six inches high, weighs 300 pounds, has two 39-inch fly-wheels and will grind three pounds of Coffee per minute, requiring only forty revolutions to grind a pound.

It is constructed from a new model, of beautiful design, and is elegantly ornamented and mounted with nickel-plated fittings.

PRICE, $50.00 ; or, with pulleys for steam-power, $60.

GRINDERS WARRANTED EQUAL TO STEEL.

ENTERPRISE
⇢❈S E L F - G A U G I N G❈⇠
CHEESE KNIFE.

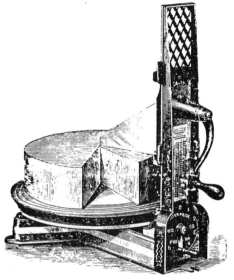

THIS machine obviates the hard labor of cutting with a hand-knife. It is not designed to cut mathematically correct as to weight, but, if a pound or more is wanted, the customer can be accommodated with ONE piece which will be within a fraction of the desired weight, instead of giving two or three pieces, or leaving yourself small pieces to dry out. It is beautifully finished in colors, ornamented with gold, and is very handsome in appearance. The blade is tinned.

DIRECTIONS FOR USE.

The cheese is first weighed and placed on the platform. By referring to the scale or table posted on the column supporting the knife, you will find opposite the number representing the weight of the cheese the number of times the SMALL crank has to be turned to measure off a pound ; then by turning the LARGE crank, the knife blade descends, cutting evenly, clearly and easily, and a pound is cut off by a single stroke.

PRICE, with Cover, $13.00.   Without Cover, $10.00.

Many serious country store collectors have searched for the Enterprise cheese knife with limited success. Our statement about country store-related items showing up in the least likely places recently came to pass for us. In a rural Alabama town eight miles from Interstate 65, we toured an antiques mall full of items in which we really had little interest. In the rear of one of the shops, surrounded by collectibles a step removed from the local landfill, was an Enterprise cheese knife. It was the only one we have ever seen for sale.

Star Threads oak display cabinet. **$550–$700**

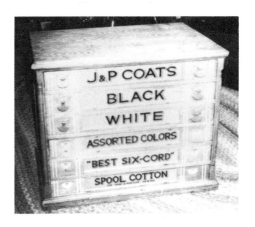

J. & P. Coats spool chest, oak. **$575–$650**

Coffee grinder from grocery store, made by Elgin, original painted finish. **$400–$650**

J. & P. Coats spool chest, oak. **$450–$600**

Chicago American newspaper street corner vendor's box. $375–$450

Counter display container for the Boye Needle Company. $250–$300

F. F. Schmalz & Sons cash register, early 1900s. $400–$550

Brass stencil for Jersey Sweet Potatoes containers. $50–$75

Sign from government building indicating days closed due to "legal holidays." c. 1915. $125–$150

"The City Candy Kitchen" tin sign, hand-lettered, framed in pine, from shop in Wisconsin, 1920s. $400–$525

Lantern made into an "Ice Cream and Pop" sign, from an Ohio general store, c. 1900. $550–$700

Tom's Toasted Peanuts counter jar, c. 1950.
$75–$100

Oak case and counter section from rural Illinois post office, c. 1920. ***$500–$600***

Collection of wooden boxes with paper labels.

Abbott's cream cheese cardboard box (small).
$15–$25

Royal Scarlet Macaroni box. **$5–$10**

Home-Canners' Jar Rubbers. **$10**

Duff's Layer Cake Mix. **$25–$30**

Jack Sprat Cherry Preserves. **$20–$25**

Canning jar rubbers: Top Flite, $4; Bull Dog, $12

Nestle's one-gallon Chocolate Flavor Syrup container. $40–$50

None So Good Butter Sweets candy display box. $75–$125

Butter Stretcher Wafers. $6–$10

Jack Frost Cinnamon and Sugar. $25–$30

Great Seal imitation banana flavoring.
$30–$35

Fiberboard African Ginger container.
$350–450

Edgar's Household Confectioners Mixture.
$12–$15

Crystal Peppo. $4–$6

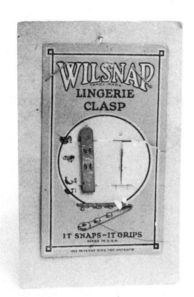

Wilsnap Lingerie Clasp. $10–$15

Hoosier Poet Cloves. $15–$20

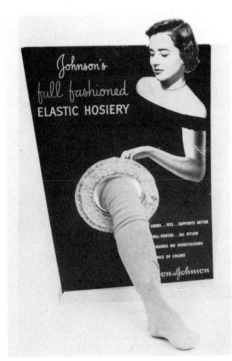

Johnson's Elastic Hosiery display. $125–$150

Snow facial depilatory. $40–$50

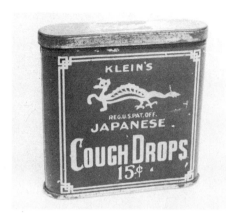

Klein's Japanese Cough Drops. $15–$20

*Putnam Soap Tints, $4 **each;** display box, $8*

Fairies ironing starch. $40–$50

Assorted razor blade packets: Keen Kutter Double Edge, $5; Gillette, $2.75; Monogram, $4; Probak, $3.25; Valet Auto-Strop, $4.25; Diamond Edge, $3.75; Gold Tone, $4; Segal, $4

Ban-Smoke Chewing Gum. $6

Pain-A-Lay antiseptic. *$8–$10*

Mother Goose shoe box. *$10–$15*

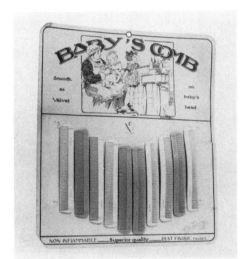

Baby's Comb complete display. *$40–$50*

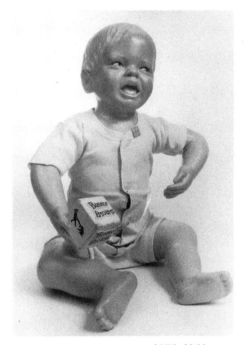

Buster Brown mannequin. *$175–$250*

Culver Cubs white baby shoes. *$25–$50*

Kenworthy's Cut-Out Letters. *$5–$10*

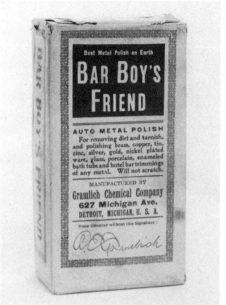

Bar Boy's Friend auto metal polish. **$15–$20**

Nu-Bowl toilet bowl cleaner. **$15–$20**

"Cool Off" Richardson's Freeze glass. **$25–$30**

Soft drink bottles: Get Up, **$5.50**; Hermann, **$12**; Bubble Up, **$4.75**

Primitive handmade wooden store display piece. $65–$75

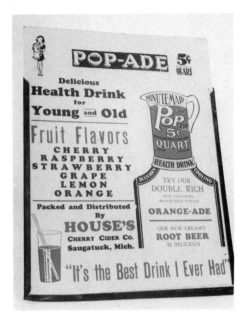

Pop-Ade advertising sign. $75–$100

Ironhose advertisement. $15–$20

Boye metal display piece for knitting needles. $40–$50

Hickory Elastic store display case. $200–$375

Hutton's Pork advertising pig. **$145–$200**

Fluffy Pancakes and Bacon advertisement. **$15–$25**

Sunkist Oranges price calculator. **$20–$25**

Paper time clock store sign. **$20–$30**

Mower's Pure Spruce Gum advertisement. **$27–$35**

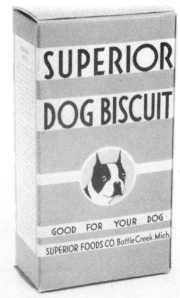

Superior Dog Biscuit box. *$20–$25*

Paperweights: Georgia Department of Labor, *$14;* Western Grocer Co. Mills, *$45–$50*

Whoopee Song Restorer and Health Food. *$14–$18*

Helena and West Helena, Arkansas, telephone book. *$10–$15*

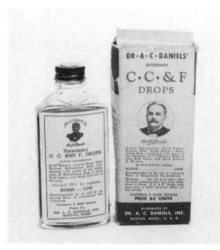

Dr. A. C. Daniels' CC & F Drops. *$15–$25*

Globe Laboratories Ko-Ex-7 Mastitis Detector.
$10–$12

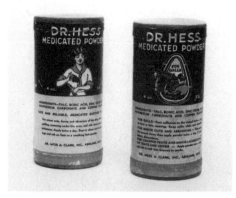

Dr. Hess Medicated Powder. *$15–$20*

Dr. David Roberts' Physic Balls horse medicine. *$10–$12*

Hero Fire Extinguishers. *$15–$20 each*

Blosser's Medical Powder. *$15–$20*

Spratt's Insect and Flea Powder. **$15–$26**

Gopher Corn poison. **$15–$20**

Hammond's Slug Shot pesticide. **$12–$15**

Acme London Purple insecticide. **$15–$20**

Den Smokers pesticide. $8

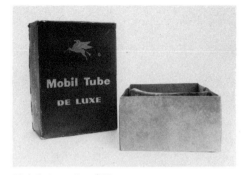

Mobil tire tube. $15

Service station items: cardboard gas price sign, $3.75; "Contains Lead" sign, $20

Alligator Steel Belt Lacing. $18–$25

Liquid Thread mending paste. $10–$12

Carter's Ink. $6

Super-X shotgun shells. $35–$50

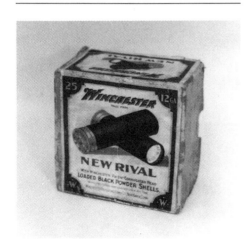

Defiance Shot Shells. $100–$125

Xpert Western Shotgun Shells. $100–$125

Pointer shotgun shells. $100–$125

Winchester New Rival shells. $50–$65

Triangle Chalk. **$2 each**

De-Linter Brush. **$9–$12**

The Boss Patent Hook Huskers. **$13 each;** *display box.* **$8**

Genuine Nails. **$8 each;** *display box.* **$5**

Souvenir decals. **$5 each**

Spalding Club Practice Shuttlecocks. **$10–$12**

Whirl-O-Halloween Fortune and Stunt Game card. $25–$30

Charlotte M. Haines seed catalog, 1937. $10–$20

Markley's African Violet Plant Food. $7–$10

Wagner Ware metal display rack for self-basting covers. $125–$135

Meyer and Faehr wooden cigar box. **$15–$20**

Polar Ice Chopper. **$20–$35**

Tissue Roping. **$13–$15**

Brilliant Aluminum Wreath. **$15–$20**

Sterling tobacco "tub" or bucket with replaced lid. $235–$250

Tennyson cigar counter display. $150– $175

T & B cigars counter display. $150–$175

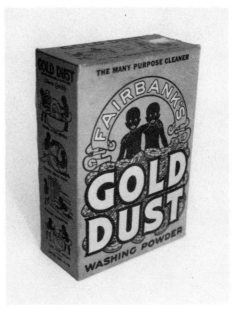

Gold Dust washing powder box. $40–$50

Indian Ax cigar box. $50–$75

Winnie Winkle cigar box. $75–$95

New Bachelor 5¢ cigars. $75–$85

College Maid cigar box. $25–$40

Texie cigar box. $125–$150

Three Beauties cigars display box. **$100–$115**

Unopened Huntress Smoking Tobacco package with tax stamp. **$85–$100**

Key West Temptation cigars box. **$100–$125**

Little Tom 5¢ cigars box. **$40–$50**

Green Lucky Strike cigarettes tin. **$35–$45**

Dixie Kid Cut Plug tobacco package. *$150–$175*

H. A. Nichols Durham Cigars, Bloomington, Ill. *$50–$75*

Mallard Cut Plug tobacco package. *$60–$70*

Lead Mine handmade cigars box, Galena, Ill. *$75–$100*

Lady Hope cigars box. *$75–$85*

Postmaster Smokers cigars tin. $45–$55

Tuscarora cigar box, Pekin, Ill. $75–$95

Circular cardboard package of Dan Patch Fine Cut tobacco. $75–$95

Unopened Oceanic Cut Plug tobacco package. $50–$65

Corn Cake Smoking tobacco. $35–$45

Pick Smoking and Chewing Tobacco, over-sized box. $125–$175

Bagley's Burley Boy tobacco. $400–$500

Bull Dog Cut Plug tobacco. ***$100–$150***

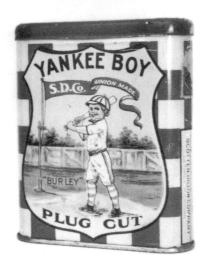

Yankee Boy Plug Cut tobacco (rare). ***$500–$600***

Sure Shot chewing tobacco package. **$25–$35**

Lutz's Frog cigar box. **$75–$85**

Peachey Scrap Chewing Tobacco box with 12 original packets. **$150–$225**

Honest Weight Tobacco package. **$75–$95**

Kildow's Panetela tin. $55–$75

Half and Half Lucky Strike tobacco tin. $35–$50

Yum Yum Smoking Tobacco tin with "drop" handle. $150–$175

Orcico cigar tin. $200–$275

Sunset Trail tobacco tin. $300–$400

"Hand Made" tobacco tin. $15–$25

Peter Hauptmann's Mixture (tobacco) tin. $15–$25

Granger pipe tobacco container. $35–$45

Tobacco packages: Navy, $35; Parrot, $65; Pep, $40; Pinch Hit, $150; Plow Boy, $45; Ramrod, $30; Red Man, $20; Scrapple, $10

Coca-Cola sign. $250–$300

Uneeda Biscuit and Graham Crackers signs. **$225–$250 each**

Goldenson Furniture sign, $35; "No Hunting" sign, **$20**

Tiger seed sign, $125; Whistle Soft Drink sign, **$55**

Metal Pinch Hit sign. **$500–$650**

American Gas globe, glass, c. 1930s.
$400–$500

Pennzoil storage rack and 8 cans.
$200–$250

Mobiloil Gargoyle rack and 24 cans.
$800–$1200

Shell motor oil storage tin, five-gallon size. *$125–$175*

137

Service station attendants' caps, c. 1940s. $60–$75 each

Texaco rest room key holder and keys, c. 1950s. $75–$85

Poll Parrot Shoe advertisement made of chalkware. $200–$250

Trade sign. $175–$225

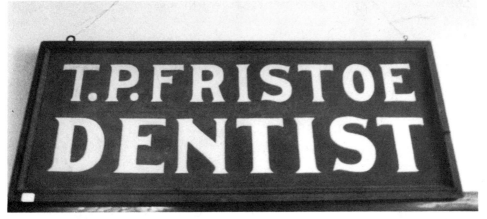

Dentist's sign. $185–$250

Saint Nicholas plaque from New Orleans theater, 36" diameter, c. early 1900s. $1200–$1300

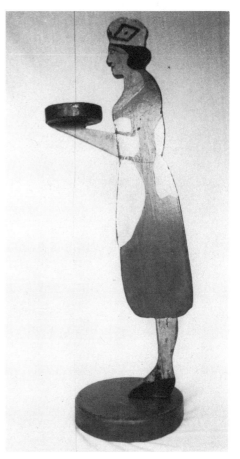

Folk art lady butler from a southern Illinois restaurant, c. 1930. $135–$150

Weatherbird Shoes cloth advertising banner. $75–$125

Salesman's sample copper wash boiler. $200–$250

Tin strainer, late nineteenth century.
$28–$35

Tin milk can for carrying to school with lunch pail. $50–$75

Wick trimmer, mid-nineteenth century.
$50–$65

Tole-painted wash bowl, c. 1850. $125–$175

Two-tube candle mold, rare form, c. 1850.
$150–$200

Circular 12-tube candle mold, rare form, mid-nineteenth century. **$900–$1200**

Pierced-tin candle lantern, c. 1860. **$400–$500**

Tin candle box, painted black, c. 1860. **$375–$450**

Pewter saucer candle holder, possibly English, c. 1840. **$125–$150**

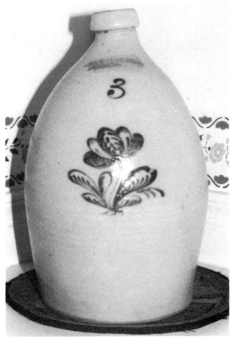

Three-gallon jug signed "John Burger, Rochester" with slip-decorated floral design. $400–$500

Four-gallon double-handled cooler signed "Cortland" with brush-decorated flower. $1200–$1600

One-half-gallon preserve jar with rare "Cortland" signature and slip- and brush-decorated flower, $350–$500; one-half-gallon unsigned preserve jar attributed to Whites, Binghamton, N.Y., decorated in blue slip, $350–$500

Six-gallon straight-sided crock signed "C. W. Braun, Buffalo, N.Y." with brush- and slip-decorated double flower. $600–$750

Four-gallon preserve jar signed "Harrington & Burger, Rochester" with slip-decorated double floral decoration. $800–$950

Three-gallon preserve jar signed "Harrington & Burger, Rochester" with slip-decorated double floral design. $800–$950

Two-gallon cream pot signed "Clark & Co., Lyons" with rare slip-decorated starburst design. $2500–$3500

Three-gallon ovoid jug signed "N. Clark, Rochester, N.Y." with vivid floral decoration. $800–$1100

Cast-iron peelers: Turntable '98 made by Goodell Co. of Antrim, N.H., pat. May 24, 1898, $125–$150; Oriole, "Scott Mfr. Co. Balt. Pat. Pend.," $400–$475

Cast-iron peelers and segmenter: clamp-on apple segmenter, "Pat. Feb. 1, 1869," a mechanical device to quarter or segment an apple, $425–$475; peach peeler, "Sinclair Scott Co. Baltimore, made in USA," $150–$175; "S.S. Hersey, Pat. June 18, '61 and Aug. 30," $225–$250

145

Raisin seeders (Rosella Tinsley Collection): Crown raisin seeder, pat. Oct. 26, 1896, $125–$150; EZY raisin seeder, pat. May 21, 1895, *$300–$350*

The Union cast-iron apple peeler, Nov. 11, 1866. $225–$250

Shaker all-wood apple peeler with attached knife, clamps onto table or bench. $1000–$1300

Improved Baystate 64 cast-iron apple peeler, made by Goodell Co., double table clamp. $225–$250

Ice cream lick glasses, $65–$85; chrome scoop, $45–$50

Whippers and beaters: Holt's Improved iron mayonnaise mixer-beater, pat. by Holt-Lyon Co. Beater apparatus affixed to Ball special glass jar, $225–$250; Archimedes' screw principle action beater, $225–$250

Old Sleepy Eye

Sleepy Eye Flour was a standard brand name in many midwestern country stores from 1883 until the Sleepy Eye Milling Company of Sleepy Eye, Minnesota (named for a Sioux Indian chief) closed in 1921. During that period, Sleepy Eye contracted with Western Stoneware Company (Monmouth, Illinois) to manufacture molded stoneware pitchers, steins, and mugs that were offered as premiums to Sleepy Eye customers. Western Stoneware continued to produce products bearing Chief Sleepy Eye's image until 1937.

Among the many Sleepy Eye related advertising products country store collectors still seek are:

> advertising or trade cards
> barrel labels
> cookbooks
> letter openers
> match holders
> paperweights
> pillow tops
> pitchers (five sizes)
> sheet music
> stationary
> steins
> spoons
> stoneware mugs (two sizes)
> thimbles
> trivets
> wooden rulers

In 1976 the Old Sleepy Eye Collector's Club (P.O. Box 12, Monmouth, IL 61462) was formed. The club offers a quarterly newsletter and an annual convention for members.

"That Sleepy Eye Flour" tin advertising sign.
$1200–$1500

"Cream" cloth flour sack. $350–$425

Flemish blue and gray stoneware vase.
$250–$325

Blue and white stoneware trivet or hot plate.
$1800–$2200

Machine-dovetailed wooden packing box.
$425–$550

Clothespin apron. **$225–$300**

Bronze letter opener. **$400–$450**

Sleepy Eye promotional fan. **$200–$250**

Back of Sleepy Eye promotional fan.

Bottom of pitcher showing Monmouth mark.

Old Sleepy Eye paperweight. $325–$385

Sleepy Eye stoneware sugar. $250–$300

Sleepy Eye stein. **$650–$750**

Sleepy Eye stein (green). **$700–$800**

Sleepy Eye bowl. **$425–$475**